Irresistible
Science
Pocket Charts

by Valerie SchifferDanoff

SCHOLASTIC
PROFESSIONAL BOOKS

New York • Toronto • London • Auckland • Sydney
Mexico City • New Delhi • Hong Kong • Buenos Aires

Dedicated to the memory of Edith Winthrop
of the Westchester Teacher Center.

I'd like to acknowledge my editor, Deborah Schecter,
for her expertise and patient assistance.

"Hibernation" by Edie Evans. Copyright © 1997 by Scholastic Professional Books. Used by permission.

"Little Seeds We Sow in Spring" from THE WINDS THAT COME FROM FAR AWAY AND OTHER POEMS by Else Holmelund Minarik.
Copyright © 1964 by Else Holmelund Minarik. Reprinted by permission of HarperCollins Publishers.

"The Painting Lesson" by Frances Greenwood and "Snow" by Lillie D. Chaffin from POETRY PLACE ANTHOLOGY.
Copyright © 1990 by Scholastic Inc. Used by permission.

"Popcorn" from A POEM A DAY by Helen H. Moore. Copyright © 1997 by Helen H. Moore. Used by permission of Scholastic, Inc.

"Stars" from STORIES TO BEGIN ON by Rhoda W. Bacmeister, published and copyright © 1940
by E. P. Dutton, Inc., New York. Used by permission.

"Sun" from 101 SCIENCE POEMS & SONGS FOR YOUNG LEARNERS by Meish Goldish.
Copyright © 1996 by Meish Goldish. Used by permission of Scholastic Inc.

Cover artwork by Vincent Ceci
Cover photographs by Donnelly Marks
Interior illustration by James Graham Hale
Interior design by Sydney Wright

ISBN: 0-439-04384-0

Contents

About This Book

Pocket charts are perfect for science. Like science, pocket charts take learning step by step. They help introduce basic concepts and provide a springboard for more in-depth learning. They both also strengthen observation skills and offer a place to record and process information.

The lessons in this book show you how to use pocket charts to enhance your science curriculum. The poems and pocket chart activities cover favorite primary science topics such as animal homes, seeds and plants, the sun and stars, and present them in ways that are educational, interactive, and fun! You'll also find hands-on activities, art projects, suggestions for research and writing, and literature links.

How to Use Pocket Charts

With a pocket chart, you can set up an instant learning center or area of focus in your classroom that is attractive, motivating, and interesting. Place activities to continue independent learning in the chart or on a table nearby, or conduct chart activities with the whole class at once. Leave the chart set up all day and use it only at science time, or use it to present and display different topics and activities throughout the school day.

Hanging and Displaying Pocket Charts

Use pocket charts anywhere in the classroom where you would like an interactive teaching space, an independent learning activity, a follow-up to a large group activity, or a learning center. Pocket charts can be displayed on a bulletin board, secured to a firm backing with heavy-duty pushpins, or clipped to an easel. Use heavy-duty Velcro® to hang pocket charts on walls or from shelves, or try pocket chart stands, available at teaching supply stores and catalogs.

You may find that pocket charts tend to roll inward when suspended. Placing a thin dowel in the bottom pocket can alleviate the problem. Most hardware and craft stores sell dowels. Cut one to the width of your chart, and place it behind the sentence strip.

When hanging pocket charts, be especially aware of the height. A wonderful feature of pocket charts is that they can hang at just the right height for young learners! Children love to be able to walk up to the chart and reach easily into a pocket.

Sizes of Pocket Charts and Sentence Strips

Pocket charts come in a variety of sizes and colors, as do sentence strips. If you cannot

afford more than one pocket chart, the most versatile size is 42 by 58 inches. This pocket chart serves as a double chart. It has ten pockets but double the space due to its width. The width can easily be divided as needed with small, blank sections of sentence strips, strips of colored masking tape, or pictures that fit in the chart. The typical pocket chart is 34 by 42 inches, also with ten pockets. A 24- by 24-inch chart is also available and is great for those smaller spaces in the classroom.

Pocket charts are mostly manufactured in blue. However, the Teaching Resource Center Catalog (1-800-833-3389) has charts in red, pink, lavender, blue, yellow, green, and white.

The best sentence strips for use in pocket charts are tagboard quality, precut to 3 by 24 inches. While rolls of sentence strips are available and cheaper, the money you save is usually not worth the aggravation of straightening them out.

Storing Sentence Strips

When storing sentence strips, you may choose to organize them by theme, skill, or concept. For easy storage, fold a large piece of cardboard in half to make a folder, then place the strips inside. A butterfly clip, large paper clip, or small clamp will keep each set of strips together.

Other containers for storing pocket strips include:
- a long-stemmed flower box,
- a box in which wallpaper comes, cut along the top,
- the box in which the sentence strips arrived, covered with contact paper,
- two manila folders, opened, folded lengthwise, and attached with tape.

Teaching Techniques for Pocket Charts

- Model proper use of pocket chart components. Teach children how to place words, sentence strips, and patterns in the pocket chart and how to carefully remove them.

- When reading from a pocket chart, read chorally with children. Point to every word as you read.

- When teaching a short poem or rhyme, encourage children to chant or repeat it. Children really enjoy this.

- Use pictures along with or instead of the words. This allows children to match words to pictures and pictures to words, sharpening reading and pre-reading skills.

- Use cutouts or stickers as manipulative materials.

- Additional techniques, hints, and reminders are presented with each pocket chart. Use these to extend and develop the lessons. Note: When preparing a pocket chart, feel free to use additional pictures from any of the lessons in this book.

Resources for Pocket Chart Supplies

Teaching Resource Center Catalog (1-800-833-3389)

School Specialty Beckley-Candy (1-888-222-1332)

Resources for Science and Poetry

June Is a Tune by Sarah Wilson. (Simon & Schuster, 1994)

101 Poems and Songs for Young Learners by Meish Goldish. (Scholastic, 1996)

The Pocket Chart Book by Valerie SchifferDanoff. (Scholastic, 1996)

Pocket Charts for Emergent Readers by Valerie SchifferDanoff. (Scholastic, 1997)

A Poem a Day by Helen H. Moore. (Scholastic, 1997)

Poetry Place Anthology (Scholastic, 1983)

Questions: Poems of Wonder selected by Lee Bennet Hopkins. (HarperTrophy, 1992)

The Random House Book of Poetry selected by Jack Prelutsky. (Random House, 1983)

Read Aloud Rhymes for the Very Young selected by Jack Prelutsky. (Alfred A. Knopf, 1986)

The Scholastic Integrated Language Arts Resource Book by Valerie SchifferDanoff. (Scholastic, 1995)

Thematic Poems, Songs, and Fingerplays by Meish Goldish. (Scholastic Professional Books, 1994)

What Can It Be? by Jacqueline A. Ball. (Simon & Schuster, 1989)

A Year of Hands-On Science by Lynne Kepler. (Scholastic, 1996)

You Be Good & I'll Be Night by Eve Merriam. (William Morrow & Co., 1988)

Tips on Teaching Science

In addition to the basic pocket chart techniques provided above, I recommend using an inquiry-based learning approach to science. Begin a study by asking children what they know about a given subject. Continue by finding out what they want to learn. Complete the activity by summing up what they have learned. Be prepared to add more questions about the subject as the children are learning. Their questions will become more specific as their knowledge base grows. The more children know, the more they want to know!

Meeting the Science Standards

The concepts in this book meet a number of the National Science Education Content Standards, the criteria intended to guide the quality of science teaching and learning in this country. The chart on page 7 shows how the topics in this book correlate with the Science Standards.

Science Education Content Standards for Grades K–4

Physical Science

- Objects have many observable properties, including size, weight, shape, color, temperature, and the ability to react with other substances.

Life Science

- Organisms have basic needs. For example, animals need air, water, and food; plants require air, water, nutrients, and light.

- Organisms can survive only in environments in which their needs can be met.

- Each plant or animal has different structures that serve different functions in growth, survival, and reproduction.

- Plants and animals have life cycles.

- Plants and animals closely resemble their parents.

- An organism's patterns of behavior are related to the nature of that organism's environment.

Earth and Space

- The sun, moon, stars, and clouds all have properties, locations, and movements that can be observed and described.

- The sun provides the light and heat necessary to maintain the Earth's temperature.

- Weather changes from day to day and over the seasons.

- Objects in the sky have patterns of movement.

Science in Personal and Social Perspectives

- Individuals have some responsibility for their own health. Students should engage in personal care—dental hygiene, cleanliness, and exercise—that will maintain and improve health.

(National Science Education Standards, National Research Council, 1996)

Animal Homes

Animal Homes

by Valerie Schiffer

A hive is a house for a bee.
Birds build nests in a tree.
Rabbits live in a hole
which also is home for a mole.
The ocean, the lake, and the bay
are where fish like to stay.
More animals live there too.
Seals, swans, and whales are a few.
Animals live on land and sea,
underground or in a tree.

Materials

- 34- by 42-inch or 42- by 58-inch pocket chart
- 11 sentence strips in two colors
- patterns (pages 11–13)
- markers
- crayons
- glue
- tagboard
- scissors

Science Focus: Animals live on land and in water.

Getting Ready

1 Write the poem on sentence strips. Alternate colors to highlight sentence pairs that rhyme. For small charts, place two lines together in one slot.

2 Photocopy and color the animal and animal home patterns. Glue these onto tagboard and cut them out.

3 Leave the sentence strips intact or cut them to set apart "home" words and "animal" words. (See Reading the Pocket Chart Poem, page 9.)

Reading the Pocket Chart Poem

1. Ask children to name some places where animals live (*in a pond, tree, cave, den,* and so on).

2. Explain that today you are going to read a poem about animal homes. Read the poem aloud. Then read it again, inviting children to join in.

3. Hand out the sentence strips and the animal and animal home patterns. If you have cut apart the home words and animal words, distribute these at the same time.

4. Ask children who hold sentence strips (or portions of them) to display them for others to see. Ask those who hold animal names and pictures to find the sentence strips that match the names or pictures they hold. (When a child displays the word *ocean*, children holding words or pictures for seals should walk over and stand near that child.) Note: While younger children may not differentiate between bodies of water, older children may specifically place animals where they belong (for example, swans in fresh water). You may want to briefly discuss this distinction.

5. Read the poem again. This time, invite children to bring their words and pictures up and place them in correct order in the chart. They will have a lot of fun coaching one another to make the correct selections.

6. Read the finished poem together.

Other Ways to Use the Poem

@ Find words that rhyme in the poem. Write them on small strips of tagboard, using a different color for each rhyming pair. Distribute these and then read the poem aloud. Let children find the rhyming words and place them in the pocket chart.

@ Ask children to help you identify word families in the poem (*-ee, -ole, -ay*). Write the words on chart paper. Ask children to name other words in the same word family and write these on the chart (*bee, see, tree, knee,* and so on).

@ Let children think of other animal homes and names to add to the poem. Write their suggestions on tagboard, and let them insert the new words in the chart. Children may want to insert their own drawings as well.

You might display the poem initially with the homes and animal names missing. As you read the poem aloud, invite those who hold the appropriate animal or home names and pictures to fill in the poem. Then reread the poem with children.

● Have children find animal words in the poem that are singular (*bee, mole*) and plural (*birds, rabbits, fish, seals, swans,* and *whales*).

Beyond the Pocket Chart

● Take a walk outside and observe animals that live near the school. Discuss where their homes might be. Invite children to try to find animal homes—for example, a bird's nest or an anthill.

● Help children learn how the characteristics of animals help determine where they make their homes. Young children may understand that since birds can fly, they nest in trees for safety. Older children may learn why penguins live in Antarctica.

● Make a temporary aquarium or terrarium in your classroom. Let it be home to animals from your environment. (Note: Carolina Biological Supply [1-800-334-5551] is a good source for fish and other small creatures.)

● Make a Venn diagram. Use the animal and animal home patterns to make a Venn diagram. On the chalkboard, draw two large circles that overlap in the center, as shown. Inside one circle, write: "Lives in Water." Inside the other, write: "Lives on Land." Let chil-

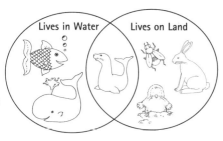

dren tape each animal inside the circle that tells where it lives. Some animals may go where the circles overlap, as they live in water and on land.

Literature ● Connections

Animals and Where They Live by John Feltwell, Ph.D. (Putnam, 1992) Hundreds of animals, their habits, and habitats are featured in this fascinating picture encyclopedia.

Nature Hide and Seek: Jungles (and others in the series) by John Norris Wood. (Random House, 1987) These lift-the-flap books introduce readers to animals that live in the woods, jungles, and other habitats.

One Small Square: Backyard by Donald M. Silver and Patricia J. Wynne. (Freeman, 1993) This book encourages readers to explore their own backyards and provides fascinating facts about the plants, animals, and insects that live there. (Part of the *One Small Square* series.)

Under Your Feet by Joanne Ryder. (Four Winds, 1990) "Under the ground, under the grass, under your feet, creatures are hiding . . ." The author takes readers on a journey of animal life over sand, up on rocks, and underwater.

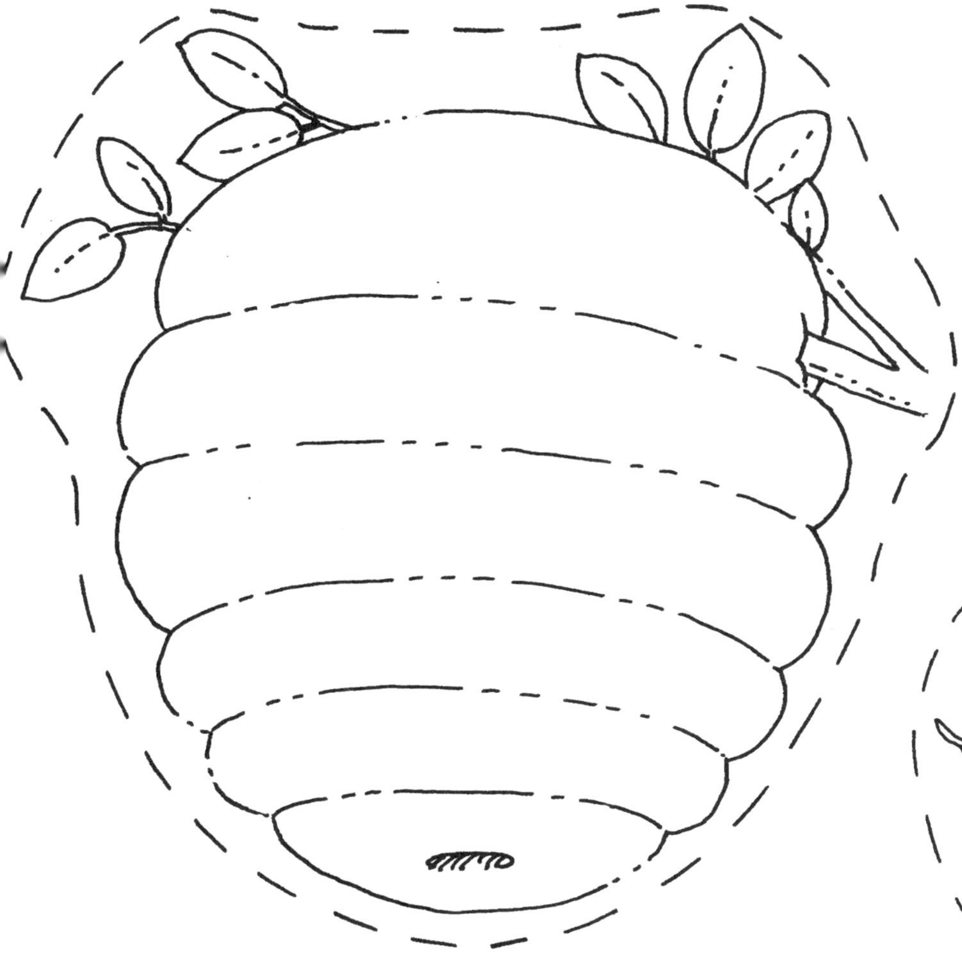

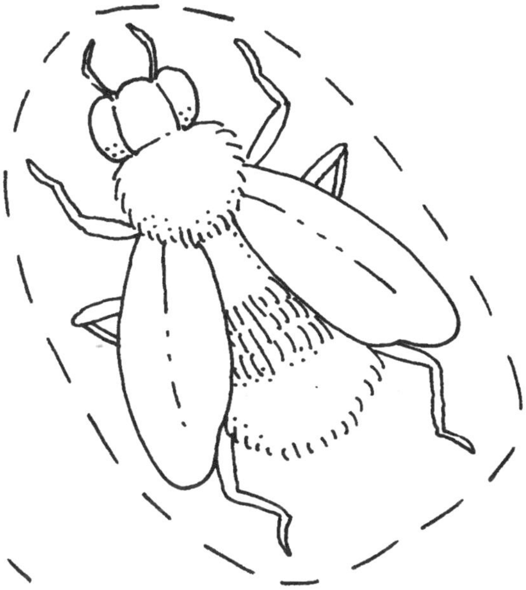

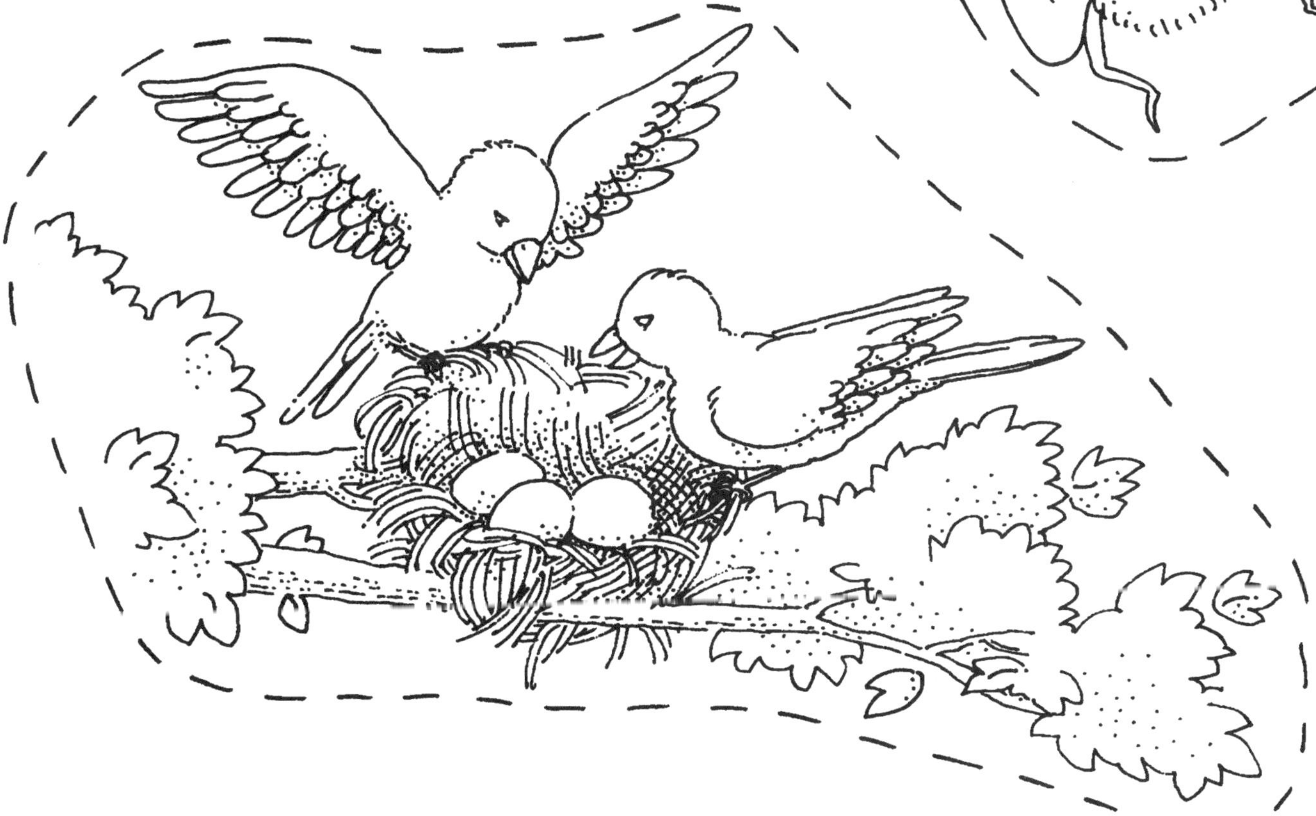

Animal Homes

Irresistible Science Pocket Charts
Scholastic Professional Books

Animal Homes

Animal Babies

Pocket Chart Poem

Who Is My Mother?

by Valerie Schiffer

When a kitten is born, it has soft, soft fur.
A cat is its mother. Listen to it purr!

A newborn joey is just one inch long.
A kangaroo is its mother. Watch her hop along!

A puppy is born with its eyes shut tight.
A dog is its mother. She feeds it day and night.

A gosling hatches from an egg and starts to eat.
A goose is its mother. It has webbed feet.

When a kit is born, it has no fur.
A rabbit is its mother. She keeps the kit with her.

This little chick has downy feathers.
A penguin is its mother. It lives in snowy weather.

Materials

- 34- by 42-inch or 42- by 58-inch pocket chart
- 19 sentence strips (13 in one color and 6 in a different color)
- adult and baby animal patterns (pages 17–20)
- markers and crayons
- tagboard and scissors
- glue

Science Focus: Animals and their young have different names.

Getting Ready

1 Write the poem on sentence strips. Leave a space for the name of each baby animal and its mother.

2 Write the animal names on strips of different colors. Cut them to size.

3 Photocopy and color the adult and baby animal patterns. Glue these onto tagboard and cut them out.

4. Place two or three animal rhymes in the pocket chart, or use a larger chart to display the whole poem. Insert the patterns of the animals and their young below the poem.

⊚ TIP ⊚

For those just developing vocabulary, display verses for familiar animals, such as dogs and cats, first. This will allow you to teach the matching process at a non-threatening level.

Reading the Pocket Chart Poem

1. Discuss with students the idea that they are *children* and their parents or guardians are *adults*. Invite them to tell what they call their parents or guardians. Explain that as parents and children have different names, so do animals and their young.

2. Read the first animal rhyme aloud. Ask children to look at the chart and find the pictures of the young animal the rhyme describes. Help them place the picture of that animal and its mother in the chart.

3. Next, help them find the matching animal names and place these in the chart to complete the verse.

4. Continue in this manner until you have read all of the rhymes displayed.

5. Ask children to name the other animals displayed in the chart but not mentioned in the rhymes (*deer/fawn*; *frog/tadpole*). Invite them to name these animals' young as well.

Other Ways to Use the Poem

⊚ Sort the Animals. Use tagboard to write the headings "Animals That Lay Eggs" and "Animals That Give Birth." Place these side by side at the top of the pocket chart. Have children sort the animal names and pictures, placing each under the appropriate heading.

⊚ Calling All Moms! Ask older children to research additional animals and the names for their young. Provide strips of tagboard, and let them add animal names and illustrations to the chart.

◎ Find Action Words. Let children locate the action words in the poem: *purr, hop, hatches, feeds.* Talk about other actions animals might do: *bark, jump, scratch, run,* and so on.

Beyond the Pocket Chart

◎ Encourage older children to make up riddles about animals and their young. Turn these into lift-the-flap books. To do this, you'll need two sheets of 8½- by 11-inch paper per child. Have each child draw a young animal on one sheet of paper. Place a second sheet on top and draw a square to mark the location of the drawing underneath it. Cut around three sides of the square to make a flap. Write a riddle on it, such as: *I have fur and I yip. A dog is my mother. Who am I?* Glue or staple around the edges to keep the two pages together. Children may wish to draw several animals on the same page, making a flap for each one.

◎ As a class or in pairs, help children conduct research to learn how various animals care—or do not care—for their young. For example, Emperor penguin parents share the care, while the sea turtle lays its eggs and crawls away. Help children share what they've learned in various ways: through drawings, dioramas, puppet shows, or talking to the group.

◎ Make a chart or Venn diagram to compare and contrast animals and their young. For example, fawns have white spots, while adult deer do not. Kits have no fur, yet their mothers have plenty.

◎ Connections

Amazing Animal Babies by Christopher Maynard. (Knopf, 1993) All kinds of animal babies appear in this colorful encyclopedia of animal young. Young readers will enjoy the detailed photographs; older readers will gain a lot from the text.

Are You My Mother? by P. D. Eastman. (Random House, 1960) A baby bird hatches in an empty nest and sets off to find its mother.

Baby Animals by Angela Royston. (Macmillan, 1992) Large, colorful pictures bring eight animal babies to life in this appealing resource for young readers.

Is Your Mama a Llama? by Deborah Guarino. (Scholastic, 1988) In riddle and rhyme, Lloyd the Llama asks each of his animal friends if their mama is a llama.

Literature

Animal Babies

Irresistible Science Pocket Charts
Scholastic Professional Books

Animal Babies

Irresistible Science Pocket Charts
Scholastic Professional Books

Animal Babies

Irresistible Science Pocket Charts
Scholastic Professional Books

Hibernation

Hibernation

by Edie Evans

Through the whole winter
a slumber so deep,
While a child counts snowflakes
a _____ is counting sheep.

Materials

- 34- by 42-inch pocket chart
- 6 sentence strips in different colors
- animal patterns (pages 24–25)
- markers
- crayons
- glue
- tagboard
- scissors

Science Focus: Some animals hibernate in winter.

Getting Ready

1 Write the poem on two different-colored sentence strips, alternating colors by line.

2 Place the strips in order in the pocket chart. Cut the last strip to divide the sentence, making room to insert an animal's name and picture.

3 Photocopy and color the animal patterns. Glue them onto tagboard and cut them out.

4 On strips of a third color, write these words: *frog, turtle, bat, groundhog, bear,* and *skunk.*

5 Place the animal patterns and their names under the poem.

Reading the Pocket Chart Poem

1 Ask children to tell what it means to hibernate. Explain that *hibernation* is a deep sleep that some animals go into when the weather gets cold. Hibernation helps protect animals' bodies from the cold and reduces the need for food, which can be hard to find in winter months.

2 Ask children to name animals that hibernate, such as bears and turtles.

3 Discuss whether animals in your region need to hibernate and why.

4 Read the poem several times. Each time, let children identify and insert a different animal name and picture.

Other Ways to Use the Poem

@ Hand out the animal names and pictures. Ask students to move to the left side of the room if they hold the name or picture of a mammal (*groundhog, skunk, bat,* and *bear*). Ask them to move to the right side if they hold the name or picture of another type of animal (*frog, amphibian; turtle, reptile*). Invite children to classify the animals in other ways such as by size, warm-blooded/cold-blooded, and so on.

@ Clap out the syllables in the name of each animal on the chart. Tally how many names have one syllable and how many have two.

@ Replace the word "snowflakes" with something else children might count in winter, such as mittens, sleigh bells, or snowmen.

Beyond the Pocket Chart

@ Discuss actions people take to keep warm in cold weather: *wear jackets and hats, turn on heat, use blankets.*

@ Assign individuals or groups the name of an animal that hibernates. Have them research and illustrate where their animal hibernates during winter. For example, bears go inside caves, while frogs burrow in mud.

@ Animal heart rates slow down during hibernation. Show students how to find their own heart rates. Help them compare their heart rates when resting and after exercising.

@ Help children list foods not available to animals in cold months (*certain green plants, fruits*). Then discuss the availability of certain seasonal foods people eat, such as watermelon and pumpkins.

@ Connections

Literature

Every Autumn Comes the Bear by Jim Arnosky. (G. P. Putnam's Sons, 1993) When the weather grows cold and snow begins to fall, a bear moves past the woodland animals and into his winter den.

One Cold Night by Claire Ewart. (G. P. Putnam's Sons, 1992) When Snow Woman comes with her blanket of snow, birds, groundhogs, and bears head for cover in their winter homes.

Wake Me in Spring by James Preller. (Scholastic, 1994) When Bear wants to sleep for the winter, even his best friend Mouse can't keep him awake.

Wintertime by Ann Schweninger. (Penguin, 1990) Heartwarming illustrations lead the way as young readers travel through the sights and sounds of winter, finding answers to even the most curious questions about the season.

Hibernation

Teeth

Teeth

by Valerie Schiffer

I've lost three teeth, but I'll grow more.
Till I've thirty-two, I'll keep score.
Sharks can lose teeth and then grow more.
Six-inch-long teeth were dinosaurs'.
I use my teeth like animals do
to chew and chew and chew and chew!

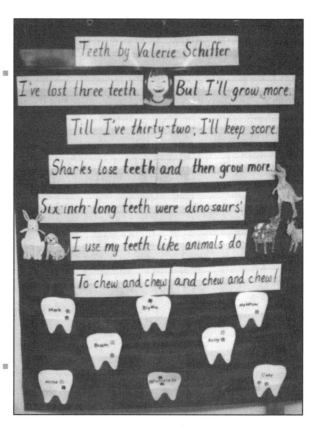

Materials

- 34- by 42-inch pocket chart
- 7 white sentence strips
- patterns (page 29)
- white tagboard
- markers and crayons
- glue
- scissors
- hand mirrors (optional)
- self-sticking notes

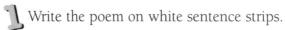

Science Focus: Our first set of teeth are replaced by permanent teeth. Teeth are important for digestion.

Getting Ready

1 Write the poem on white sentence strips.

2 Trace and cut a tooth from white tagboard for each child.

3 Photocopy and color the grinning child, Tyrannosaurus Rex, and shark patterns. Glue onto tagboard and cut them out.

4 Place the sentence strips and patterns in the chart.

Reading the Pocket Chart Poem

1. Have children count the number of teeth in each other's mouths. (Have hand mirrors available for children to look in their own mouths.) Compare their results. Then explain that most adults have 32 teeth, but most children have 10 to 20 on the bottom and 10 on the top.

2. Ask children to raise hands if they have lost any teeth. Invite volunteers to tell why children lose their teeth. Then explain that children's first set of teeth (baby teeth) are very small. As children grow, a larger set of teeth (permanent teeth) grow in. As permanent teeth grow, they push out baby teeth.

3. Read the poem aloud. Then read it a second time with children.

4. Ask children why they need teeth. Talk about the idea that teeth are very important because they help us chew food into small pieces so our bodies can use it. Chewing is one of the first steps in food digestion.

5. Invite children to think about babies and the kinds of foods they eat. Why do babies eat applesauce, soft cereals, and other soft foods? Help children understand that without teeth, babies cannot bite or chew foods.

6. Help children point out which of their own teeth they use to bite and which they use to chew.

Other Ways to Use the Poem

- Scramble the sentences strips. Let children put the poem back in order.

- On self-sticking notes, write the names of children and the number of teeth they've lost (including those who have lost none). Then cover the number in the first line of the poem with a child's name and the number of teeth he or she has lost. Also replace pronouns where necessary. Reread the revised rhyme. For example, *Peter has lost two teeth, but he'll grow more.*

- Replace the first two lines of the poem with number sentences for children to solve. Examples:
  - I had 20 teeth. I lost 3. How many teeth do I have?
  - I lost 3 teeth. Then I lost 2 more. How many teeth did I lose in all?

Ask children to think of other uses for teeth besides chewing, such as biting, smiling, chattering, and helping form letter sounds. Write these words on tagboard strips. Let children put the strips on the pocket chart in place of the word "chew."

Beyond the Pocket Chart

Here's a great activity to begin in September and carry on all year. Write each child's name on a tagboard tooth and post the teeth in your classroom. Each time a child loses a tooth, place a sticker on the tagboard tooth and write the date.

Use food to investigate which teeth bite and which chew. Give each child one section of an apple to eat. (First check for any food allergies.) Ask: "Which teeth do you use to bite the apple? Which teeth do you use to chew it?" Try this with other kinds of food, too. Chewing gum, for instance, goes right to the molars.

Invite children to tell how they care for their teeth: by eating healthful foods, brushing and flossing, and visiting the dentist. As a class, write and illustrate rules for tooth care. Post them on the pocket chart.

Help children realize that teeth are actually clues to an animal's diet. With your help, have children conduct research to find out animals that eat meat and animals that eat plants. Note that meat-eating dinosaurs, such as Tyrannosaurus Rex, had long, sharp teeth for tearing meat. Plant-eating animals such as cows have flat teeth. Have children draw pictures of meat-eaters and plant-eaters. Then classify them on the pocket chart.

Connections

Literature

Arthur's Tooth by Marc Brown. (Little Brown, 1985) Arthur can't wait for his first tooth to fall out and tries hard to speed up the process.

How Many Teeth? by Paul Showers. (HarperCollins, 1991) Sam and his friends count their teeth and wiggle the loose ones while readers learn about teeth and the transition from baby teeth to permanent.

My Loose Tooth by Stephen Krensky. (Random House, 1999) In this entertaining early reader, a young boy tries hard to get his loose tooth to fall out.

What Big Teeth You Have! by Patricia Lauber. (HarperCollins, 1986) Is the bark really worse than the bite? In some cases, yes! This book takes a look at animals and their teeth, showing how the size, shape, and number of teeth affect an animal's diet and lifestyle.

Teeth

Irresistible Science Pocket Charts
Scholastic Professional Books

Popcorn

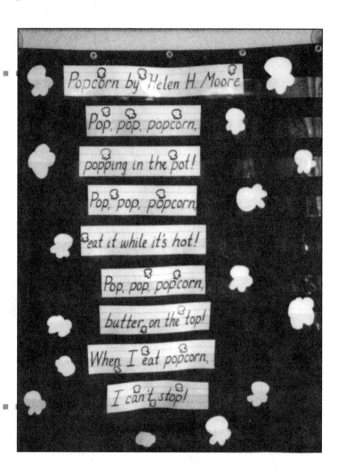

Pocket Chart Poem · · · ·

Popcorn

by Helen H. Moore

Pop, pop, popcorn,
popping in the pot!
Pop, pop, popcorn,
eat it while it's hot!
Pop, pop, popcorn,
butter on the top!
When I eat popcorn,
I can't stop!

Materials

- 34- by 42-inch pocket chart
- 9 white sentence strips
- black permanent marker
- popcorn patterns (page 31)
- white tagboard
- scissors
- popcorn, popped and unpopped

Science Focus: Heat makes popcorn pop.

Getting Ready

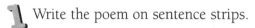

1 Write the poem on sentence strips.

2 Photocopy the popcorn pattern. Trace and cut out several pieces of popcorn.

3 Place the sentence strips in the chart. Then insert popcorn patterns as if they are popping around the poem.

Reading the Pocket Chart Poem

1 Before beginning, be sure you have enough popcorn to go around.

2 Ask children to tell what popcorn is and why they think it is called popcorn.

3 Invite them to tell how popcorn looks before it pops and how it changes after heating.

4 Read the poem once. Then reread it with your class.

5 Children might enjoy popping up like popcorn as you read. Let them take turns standing in front of the class in groups to imitate popcorn as the class reads the poem. Have children pop up at different times the way popcorn does.

6 Ask the class what they think causes popcorn to pop. List their ideas on a chart. Then explain that popcorn pops because there is a tiny droplet of water sealed inside each kernel. When the kernel gets hot, the water inside turns to steam, causing the kernel to expand and burst.

7 Give each child a handful of popcorn to eat and enjoy! (Check for food allergies beforehand.) Then read the poem again, as a class.

Other Ways to Use the Poem

© Have children find the rhyming words in the poem. Write these on small strips of tagboard, using a different color for each rhyming pair or trio (*pot/hot, pop/top/stop*). Let children place the words where they belong in the pocket chart.

© Read the poem aloud and clap the tempo of each line. Children may notice that the line "Pop, pop, popcorn" is clapped slowly, while the line that follows it is clapped briskly. Provide drums, rhythm sticks, and triangles. Let children match the rhythm of the poem as they read.

- Show children what an exclamation point is, and explain that it is used to add excitement or enthusiasm to a sentence. Help them locate one in the poem and then count the number of exclamation points in all (four). You may want to have children change the poem to end sentences with question marks (Pop, pop, popcorn. Is it popping in the pot?), or periods. (Pop, pop, popcorn is popping in the pot.)

Beyond the Pocket Chart

- Make popcorn as a class using a hot-air popper or a covered pot, oil, and hot plate (adult use only).

- Using a balance scale, compare the weight of unpopped and popped kernels. First, show children the two kinds of kernels and ask them to predict which will tip the scale more. Start by placing a few kernels of unpopped popcorn on one side of the scale and an equal number of popped kernels on the other side. If you have more than one balance scale available, let children work in small groups and compare their findings. How many popped kernels did it take to balance the unpopped?

- Practice estimation by asking children to predict how many pieces of popped popcorn they will need to fill an eight-ounce paper cup. Write children's guesses on the bottoms of their cups. Then let them fill their cups and count the kernels. Try the same activity with unpopped kernels. Use four-ounce cups, and count kernels by tens.

- Read *The Popcorn Book* by Tomie de Paola. (Holiday House, 1978). Invite children to write their own legends about popcorn. Enlarge the popcorn pattern and use it to make shape books for the stories.

Connections

Literature

Popcorn at the Palace by Emily Arnold McCully. (Harcourt Brace, 1997) In the mid-1800s, an American farmer and his daughter travel to England to introduce popcorn to Queen Victoria and Prince Albert.

The Popcorn Shop by Alice Low. (Scholastic, 1993) When Nell can't make popcorn fast enough to satisfy her customers, she invests in a giant popping machine. Now there's too much popcorn, and it's filling up the town!

Seeds and Plants

Little Seeds We Sow in Spring

by Else Holmelund Minarik

Little seeds we sow in spring
growing while the robins sing,
give us carrots, peas and beans,
tomatoes, pumpkins, squash and greens.
And we pick them,
one and all,
through the summer,
through the fall.
Winter comes, then spring, and then
little seeds we sow again.

Materials

- 34- by 42-inch or 42- by 58-inch pocket chart
- 11 sentence strips in a variety of colors
- patterns (pages 36–37)
- crayons and markers
- glue
- tagboard
- scissors
- chart paper
- clothespins

Science Focus: Seeds grow into plants.
Seasonal changes affect plant growth.

Getting Ready

1. Write the poem on sentence strips of different colors. You may want to use the colors in the same sequence as a rainbow (red, orange, yellow, green, blue, violet). Or use pastels for a spring-like display.

2. Photocopy and color the patterns. Glue them onto tagboard and cut them out.

3. Place the sentence strips in the pocket chart. Put the patterns below the poem.

Reading the Pocket Chart Poem

1. Ask children: "What is a seed?" List their responses on the chalkboard.

2. Ask whether any of the children have ever helped plant a garden. If so, invite them to tell at what time of year they helped plant and what time of year the plants were full-grown. This may lead into a discussion of seasons. Briefly review them.

3. Read the poem aloud. Help children understand what it means to sow a seed. Then encourage them to read the poem with you. As they read, young children may enjoy acting out sowing seeds, seeds growing, and picking plants.

4. Help children locate the names of fruits and vegetables in the poem. Let them find the pattern that illustrates each one and place it near its name. (Note: There is not a pattern for the squash.)

Other Ways to Use the Poem

Go through the poem with children and locate the names of the four seasons. Review their order in the calendar year: winter, spring, summer, fall. Write the four names on chart paper. Invite children to read through the poem and tell what they've learned about each season. Write their words on the chart under the appropriate season. Next, invite children to share what they already know about each season, and add their ideas to the chart. (*Snow falls in winter, leaves change color in fall,* and so on.)

spring	sow seeds
summer	pick peas
fall	pick squash
winter	comes before spring

Make a graph to find out which fruit or vegetable is most popular with your class. Place the fruit and vegetable patterns in a column down one side of the pocket chart. Ask children to tell which they like best. Clip a clothespin on the chart to mark each child's vote. Count the clothespins in each row to tally votes.

Beyond the Pocket Chart

Give each child a paper towel, a lima bean that has soaked overnight, and a hand lens. Instruct children to gently rub the bean between a thumb and forefinger to open it. Inside they will see the "baby" plant getting ready to grow. Have them place it on the table and examine it with the hand lens.

Give each child a paper towel and a sealable plastic sandwich bag on which you have written his or her name with a permanent marker. Instruct children to fold the towel so it lines the bottom of the bag. (Most towels folded in half three times will do the trick.) Using water from a measuring cup, help children moisten their towels. Then have each child place three dried peas along the bottom of the bag. Clip the bags to the pocket chart or to a nearby wall. Avoid placing them in direct sun, and be sure to keep the towels moist. Very soon, the peas will sprout and grow!

Provide an assortment of dried seeds. (Many hardware stores sell packaged seeds ten for $1.00; grocery stores sell inexpensive bags of dried beans.) Give each child a paper plate and liquid glue. Invite children to make a seed picture or collage.

Demonstrate the idea that people eat all parts of plants, from roots to leaves to seeds. Bring in a variety of fruits and vegetables, such as carrots and potatoes (*roots*), celery (*stem*), lettuce and parsley (*leaves*), peas and sunflower seeds (*seeds*), bananas and oranges (*fruit*), and broccoli (*flower*). Encourage children to taste the fruits and vegetables and/or to identify those they eat at home. Talk about the different ways fruits and vegetables are prepared. Some, such as oranges, can be squeezed to make juice. Others, such as lettuce, are torn into pieces and eaten. Potatoes can be boiled, baked, or fried.

Safety Note: Check for food allergies before doing this activity.

⟡TIP⟡

Children can observe and record the whole process in a bean journal, through writing and drawing.

⟡ Connections

Literature

The Big Seed by Ellen Howard. (Simon & Schuster, 1993) When little Bess plants a seed for a school project, she grows a BIG surprise.

In My Garden by Helen Oechsli and Kelly Oechsli. (Macmillan, 1985) In this handbook for young gardeners, the authors offer advice on growing seven different vegetables.

Mouse and Mole and the Year-Round Garden by Doug Cushman. (Freeman, 1994) Two friends work in their garden and learn how the seasons affect sowing, growing, and harvest.

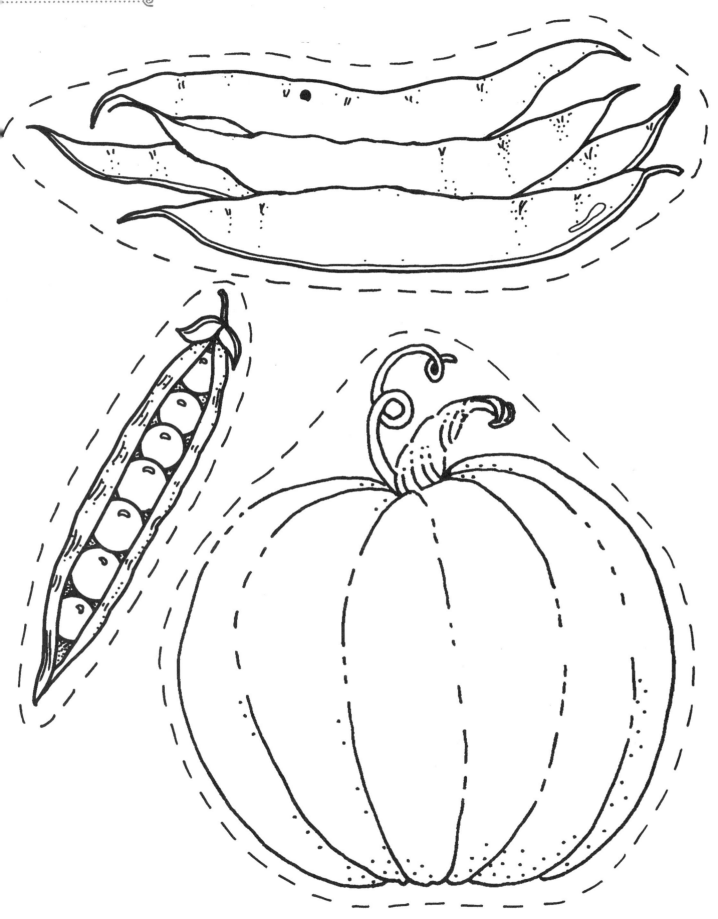

Irresistible Science Pocket Charts
Scholastic Professional Books

Trees and Leaves

Riddle-a-Tree

by Valerie Schiffer

I have pointy needles,
but they're not for sewing.
I have crisp brown cones,
but no ice cream showing.
(spruce)

You love the syrup
made from my sap.
My pointy leaves give you
shade for a nap.
(sugar maple)

I drop lots of acorns,
they are very small.
I can grow up to be
50 feet tall.
(red oak)

My leaves are slender.
My bark is gray.
My nuts turn brown
on summer days.
(beech)

Materials

- 34- by 42-inch pocket chart
- 18 sentence strips in five different colors
- patterns (pages 41–42)
- black marker
- colored markers or crayons
- tagboard
- glue
- scissors

Note: It is helpful to have a tree guide on hand for this lesson. (See Literature Connections, page 40.)

Science Focus: Leaves come in different shapes and sizes.

Getting Ready

1. Write the riddles on sentence strips, omitting the answers. Use different colors to distinguish one set of riddles from another.

2. Write the following tree names on sentence strips of a different color: *red oak, sugar maple, beech, spruce, palm,* and *sweet gum.* Cut apart the words.

3. Photocopy and color the leaf patterns listed above. Then glue them onto tagboard and cut them out.

4. Place two riddles and the six leaf patterns and tree names listed in step 2 in the pocket chart.

Reading the Pocket Chart Poem

1 Read each riddle aloud. Then invite the children to read it with you.

2 Discuss the characteristics of each tree described in the riddle. Compare them with the leaves in the chart.

3 Help children match the correct leaf to each riddle.

4 Replace the first set of riddles with the remaining ones. Repeat steps 1 to 3.

Other Ways to Use the Poem

© Let each child choose one word from the poem to illustrate. Have children use crayons or markers to draw on squares of tagboard. Insert each picture over its word in the pocket chart, and read the poem together as a rebus.

© Help children make up their own riddles to add to the chart. Trees they might write about include palms, ginkos, and sassafras. (Additional leaf patterns are included on page 42.) Write the riddles on tagboard strips and place them in the pocket chart.

© Write the riddles on a second set of sentence strips. Cut each sentence into sections and distribute these. Ask the children to place them in the pocket chart, correctly joining the parts of each sentence and putting each rhyme in proper order.

Beyond the Pocket Chart

© Go on a walk to find and collect leaves on the ground. Use a tree guide to identify the leaves and trees you see. Back in the classroom, help children group the leaves by size, shape, color, and points. If any leaves are different from the ones shown on the pocket chart, trace them onto

tagboard. Cut out each leaf and place in the pocket chart beside a label that tells its name.

Make leaf rubbings by placing a leaf under newsprint and rubbing over it with the side of a crayon. Have children compare and contrast the leaves by size and shape.

Broaden children's awareness of the part trees play in their lives. Brainstorm with them to make a list of products that people get from trees, such as wood to build furniture and houses, fibers to make clothing and bedding, latex to make rubber boots and tires, and medicines used in health care. Trees also provide food in the form of fruits, nuts, chocolate, coffee, syrup, gum, and spices.

Connections

Literature

A Busy Year by Leo Lionni. (Alfred A. Knopf, 1992) Two mice befriend a tree and watch it change throughout the seasons.

National Audubon Society First Field Guide: Trees by Brian Cassie. (Scholastic, 1999) This easy-to-use guide includes full-color photographs of trees, their leaves, seeds, and fruits.

Once There Was a Tree by Natalia Romanova. (Penguin, 1983) An old stump and a new tree attract creatures who need trees for various reasons.

Picture Guide to Tree Leaves by Raymond Wiggers. (Watts, 1981) This handbook identifies dozens of trees and their leaves with informative text and large, colorful photos.

Why Do Leaves Change Color? by Betsy Maestro. (HarperCollins, 1994) The process of leaves changing color is explained in vivid pictures and text.

Trees and Leaves

sugar maple

beech

spruce

red oak

Irresistible Science Pocket Charts
Scholastic Professional Books

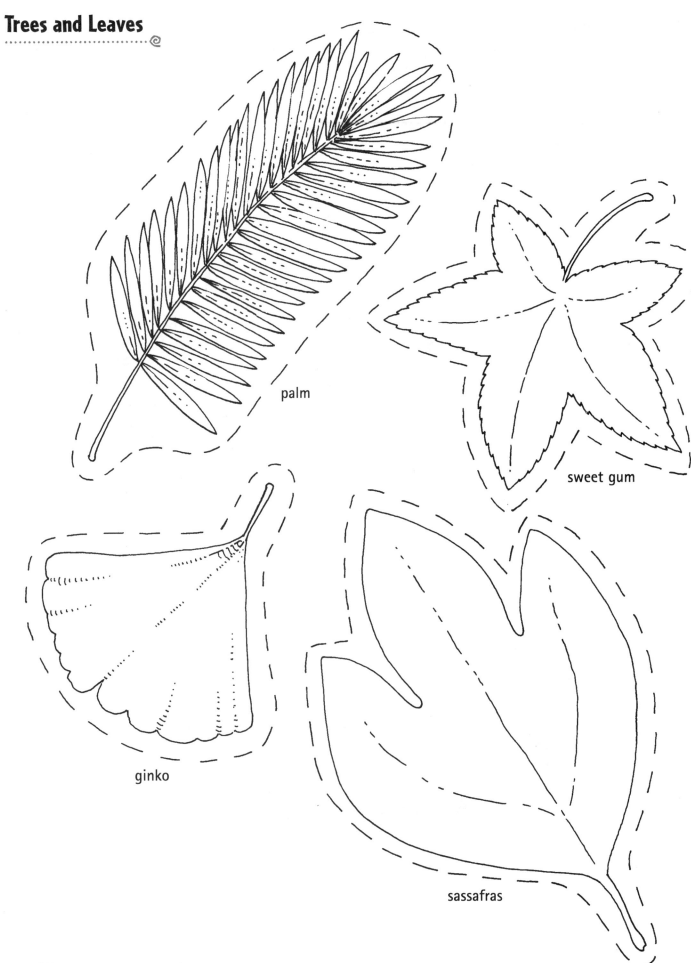

palm

sweet gum

ginko

sassafras

Sun

Sun

by Meish Goldish

If I were the sun,
I'd have such fun!
I'd shine so bright
on everyone.
I'd be a ball
of glowing gas.
I'd be a star
with giant mass!
I'd warm the plants,
I'd warm the earth.
I'd show how much
my rays are worth!

Materials

- 34- by 42-inch or 42- by 58-inch pocket chart
- 13 sentence strips
- small easel clips
- patterns (pages 46–47)
- markers and crayons
- glue
- scissors
- tagboard
- two-sided sticky tape
- colored construction paper, one sheet per child
- tagboard patterns for tracing (triangles, stars, circles)

Science Focus: The sun is the star nearest our planet. A star gives off its own light.

Getting Ready

1. Write the poem on sentence strips. You may want to alternate colors to stress the end rhymes.

2. Photocopy and color the patterns. Then glue them onto tagboard and cut them out.

3. Place the sentence strips and patterns face down in the chart (blank side showing).

4. Place the pocket chart near or opposite a window.

Reading the Pocket Chart Poem

1 Ask children to describe the sun using one word. Write their words on chart paper (for example, *bright, warm, big, hot, star*).

2 Ask children what they know is true about the sun. Write these ideas on the same paper. (*It is bright; it is warm; it is up in the sky; it moves throughout the day.*)

3 Turn over the sentence strips. As you do so, ask children to identify words in the poem that match their words and statements about the sun.

4 Read the poem with your class.

5 Review ideas in the poem that the children may not understand, such as the idea that the sun is a ball of glowing gas, that it is a star, and that it is very big. (Note: While these concepts are difficult for young children to grasp, this discussion will help build a foundation for future explorations and understanding.)

6 Discuss how important the sun is to our Earth: It provides heat and light. Emphasize the idea that without the sun's heat and light, there would be no life on Earth.

7 Hand out the patterns of the sun, Earth, star, and flower. Read the poem aloud again. This time, let children place the patterns in the chart as you read.

Other Ways to Use the Poem

● Invite children to find the rhyming words in the poem (*sun/fun/everyone, gas/mass, earth/worth*). Write the words on small strips of tagboard, in different colors for each rhyming set. Read the poem again with children. Let volunteers take turns placing each rhyming word in the poem as they read it aloud.

● Use your pocket chart to conduct an experiment with the sun. Here's what to do:

• Make a selection of patterns of the sun, Earth, star, and flower by tracing the ones on pages 46 and 47 onto tagboard. Children can use these for tracing.

- Give each child one sheet of construction paper (cut in half widthwise), a pair of scissors, and a tagboard pattern to trace.

- Have each child trace the pattern onto one half of the paper and cut it out.

- Use tape to gently attach the shape each child has traced to the center of the other piece of paper.

- Clip children's papers to the pocket chart, and leave the chart in the sun for several days.

- After a few days, have children check their "sun prints" by lifting each shape off its backing.

- Encourage children to observe and comment on how the part of the construction paper covered by the shape is darker than its border.

- You may want to have children make more than one setup and compare them based on the number of days spent in the sun.

Beyond the Pocket Chart

Talk about the sun's power: how it heats up the earth, air, and water. Then, if the weather is warm and sunny, demonstrate the heating power of the sun on a small scale. Distribute a three-inch square of aluminum foil to each child, along with four or five pieces of broken crayons. Have each child place the crayons on the foil and then place the foil on the ground outside. (In windy weather, place foil inside an open box where it is exposed to sun but will not blow away.) Leave the crayons in the sun for most of the day, until they have melted in the heat. Ask children to describe the changes they observe.

Discuss shadows. Explain that shadows happen when a shape blocks the sun's rays. When making sun prints, the sun's rays were blocked by the shape. To make human shadows, children need only stand between the sun and a wall or the ground. Let children experiment with sun shadows on a sunny day.

Safety Note: Caution children to never look directly at the sun.

⊜ Connections

Literature

Bawshou Rescues the Sun: A Han Folktale by Chun-Chan Yeh and Allan Baillie. (Scholastic, 1991) When the King of the Devils steals the sun, Bawshou embarks on a magical journey to bring it back.

The Sun Is Always Shining Somewhere by Allan Fowler. (Children's Press, 1991) This book studies the sun and compares it to other stars far away.

Sun Up, Sun Down by Gail Gibbons. (Harcourt Brace Jovanovich, 1983) Characteristics of the sun and its effects on the earth are described in this interesting picture book.

Why the Sun and the Moon Live in the Sky by Elphinstone Dayrell. (Houghton Mifflin, 1987) After the sun invites the sea to visit, the sun and the moon must leave their homes.

Sun

Irresistible Science Pocket Charts
Scholastic Professional Books

Stars

Stars

by Rhoda W. Bacmeister

Bright stars, light stars
Shining-in-the-night stars,
little twinkly, winkly stars,
deep in the sky.

Yellow stars, red stars,
shine-when-I'm-in-bed stars,
oh how many blink stars,
far, far away!

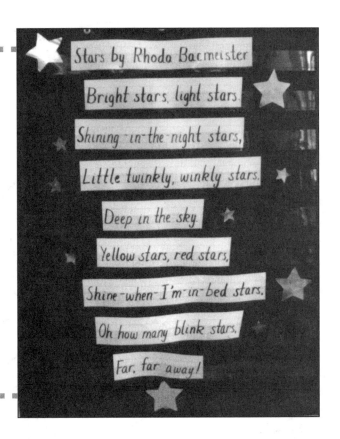

 **Materials**

- 34- by 42-inch pocket chart
- 9 sentence strips
- star pattern (page 46)
- markers
- tagboard (gold or silver; yellow and green)
- scissors
- art supplies (crayons, glue and glitter, clay, collage materials)
- drawing paper, poster-board, craft paper, or a shoebox

Science Focus: Stars are points of light in the night sky. Stars come in different sizes and colors.

Getting Ready

1 Write the poem on sentence strips.

2 Use the star template to trace and cut out stars from tagboard. (Gold or silver makes an attractive display.)

3 Place the sentence strips and the stars in the pocket chart.

Reading the Pocket Chart Poem

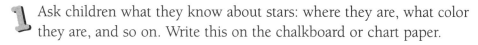

1 Ask children what they know about stars: where they are, what color they are, and so on. Write this on the chalkboard or chart paper.

2 Read the poem aloud. Then invite children to read it with you.

3 Direct their attention to the second verse. Ask: "What colors does this poem tell us stars can be?" Explain that just as some stars look white, or yellow, like the sun, others glow red or blue.

4 Invite children to review the poem and note other facts about stars, such as:

- They can be seen at night. (*Stars shine day and night, yet they can only be seen in a dark, clear sky.*)

- Stars are far, far away.

- Some stars appear to twinkle. (*Starlight comes to Earth through moving air.*)

- Some stars shine brighter than others.

Write their observations on the chart.

Other Ways to Use the Poem

Have children find the adjectives in the poem. Write these on strips of yellow tagboard. Let children place them in the pocket chart over the words they match. Then ask children to think of synonyms—words that mean the same thing—for each adjective. Write these on strips of green tagboard and place them in the pocket chart over the original words. For example, instead of *bright* and *light*, children might put *shiny* and *faint*.

Read the poem aloud with children. Point to each word on the pocket chart as they clap out the rhythm of the poem.

Divide the class into small groups. Assign each group either the first or second verse of the poem. Ask children to illustrate that portion of the poem using art supplies such as markers and paints, glitter and glue, clay, collage materials, and so on. Choose a backdrop for each group to work with, such as posterboard, craft paper, or a shoebox.

Beyond the Pocket Chart

Let children create their own starry scenes with black construction paper and star stickers.

- Punch holes in tagboard to make constellation stencils. Let children place stencils over paper and put stickers in place through the holes.

- Let children use the stickers to create their own constellations. Have them connect the stars with chalk, name the constellation, and write or dictate a story about it.

- Ask older children to re-create actual constellations. (See patterns and Literature Connections, page 51.)

Have children use the star template to trace and cut out stars for a mobile. Provide sequins and glitter glue for decoration.

Have each child trace the star template six times on drawing paper. Place the six stars in a pile and staple them together to make a shape book. Inside their books, have children write or dictate six facts they've learned about stars.

Encourage children to go outside at night with a parent or guardian and look up at the stars. You may want to suggest a location from which a full view of the night sky is available.

Make a constellation viewer for the classroom. Here's how:

- Photocopy the pattern for the Big Dipper on page 51. Cut it out and place it on a sheet of black construction paper.

- Place this on top of several layers of folded newspaper.

- Use a straight pin to poke holes in the pattern.

- Remove the pattern, and place only the black paper over one end of a paper towel tube. Be sure the star pattern is centered over the tube's opening. Secure it with tape or a rubber band.

- Dim the classroom lights. Shine a flashlight into the uncovered end of the paper towel tube, and point the tube at the wall to cast the constellation for all to see.

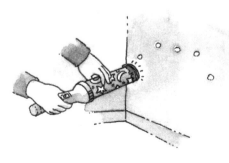

NOTE: Older children may be able to make their own viewers, if you feel comfortable with them using pins. If so, make multiple copies of the constellation patterns on page 51 and let each child pick one to use. Then provide each child with the same materials you used to make your viewer.

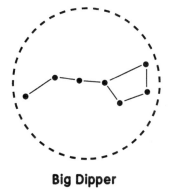

Big Dipper

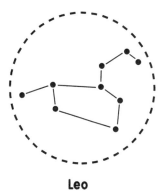

Leo

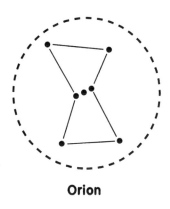

Orion

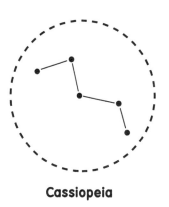

Cassiopeia

Connections

Literature

Find the Constellations by H. A. Rey. (Houghton Mifflin, 1988) This guide to the stars describes constellations as they appear throughout the year and tells how to identify them.

Her Seven Brothers by Paul Goble. (Bradbury, 1984) In this retelling of a Cheyenne legend, a girl and her seven brothers become the Big Dipper.

Sky All Around by Anna Hines. (Clarion, 1989) A father and daughter step into the night together and spend a special evening watching the stars.

Stargazers by Gail Gibbons. (Holiday House, 1992) This informative book tells what stars are, why they twinkle, how the constellations were named, and more.

Rain

Pocket Chart Poem

Rain On

by Valerie Schiffer

Rain on the green grass
and rain on the tree
Rain on the housetop
but not on me.
Rain on the flowers
and rain on the bees
Rain on the umbrella
but not on me!

Materials

- 34- by 42-inch
  pocket chart
- 9 blue sentence strips
- permanent markers
  and crayons
- patterns (pages 55–56)
- tagboard
- glue
- scissors
- drawing paper

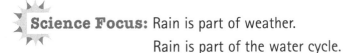
Science Focus: Rain is part of weather.

Rain is part of the water cycle.

Getting Ready

1 Write the poem on sentence strips.

2 Photocopy and color the patterns. Then glue them onto tagboard and cut them out.

3 Place the sentence strips in the pocket chart. Keep the patterns out of the chart for now.

Reading the Pocket Chart Poem

1. Ask children what they do to stay dry in the rain (*put on raincoats, open umbrellas,* and so on).

2. Hand out the patterns. Read the poem aloud once. Then invite children to read it with you. Let volunteers insert the patterns near the words that name them.

3. Ask children to look at the poem and tell where the rain fell: on the grass, trees, housetops, flowers, bees, and even the umbrella. Invite them to tell which of these plants, animals, or objects need rain.

4. Help children understand that *all* living things need rain, including people. Rain provides water to help grass, trees, and flowers grow. It provides water for people and animals to drink. Even nonliving things benefit from rain, as it washes everything it touches, including air.

Other Ways to Use the Poem

- Using the poem as a model, ask children to write their own poems about rain. Let children write these on strips of tagboard or construction paper and take turns displaying their poems in the chart.

- Ask children to choose one of the plants, animals, or objects from the poem. Have them write or draw how it feels to be rained on.

Beyond the Pocket Chart

- Demonstrate the idea behind rainfall. Dip a large sponge into a bowl of water. Explain that the sponge is like a cloud that has absorbed water from the earth. The cloud is full and heavy with water. Let children guess what happens when a cloud becomes this way. Squeeze the sponge, letting the water drop into the bowl, just as raindrops fall from a cloud to the earth.

- On a rainy day, place several containers outside, away from trees and buildings, to collect rainwater. After one day, bring the containers inside. Dip a ruler into each container to measure the water level, and record this on a bar graph. Repeat this activity on several rainy days. Let

children graph all results to compare rainfall. Keep the rainwater you collect. Let children examine it to see if it is clean.

◎ Ask children why some things get wet in the rain, while others appear not to get wet. Have they ever run for cover under a big tree or noticed during a brief shower that some areas stay dry? Explain that some objects shelter others from rain. Demonstrate this by going outside after it rains. Help your class find dry spots on the ground. Lift up wet leaves, logs, and stones to find dry ground underneath.

◎ Study the water cycle. Explain that all water on Earth has been here a long time. It is used again and again through the water cycle. Help children understand that water evaporates into the air and is absorbed by clouds. When clouds get heavy, they let go of some water, and it falls back to Earth, filling up oceans, rivers, puddles, and other bodies of water. Let children observe this by going outside just after a heavy rain. Let children find puddles and jump over them. To help them better understand the concept of evaporation, mark the perimeter of a puddle with chalk. Then return over the next few days to observe how the puddle has shrunk, until it eventually disappears.

◎ Connections

Literature

Bringing the Rain to Kapiti Plain by Verna Aardema. (Dial, 1981) Ki-pat of Kenya brings rain to the drought-stricken African plain in this story-told-in-rhyme.

The Cloud Book by Tomie de Paola. (Holiday House, 1975) What are clouds and what do they do? The author/illustrator introduces the ten most common clouds, discusses the myths they inspire, and tells how they affect the weather.

Rain Talk by Mary Serfozo. (Macmillan, 1990) A child enjoys a delightful day in the rain, listening to the sounds of the rainfall.

Water by Gallimard Jeunesse and Pierre-Marie Valat. (Scholastic, 1990) With the help of transparent overlays, water is presented in various forms.

Rain

Irresistible Science Pocket Charts
Scholastic Professional Books

Rain

Irresistible Science Pocket Charts
Scholastic Professional Books

Snow

Snow

by Lillie D. Chaffin

Snow blows
in bunches.
Snow sparkles
and crunches.

Snow is clean and cold.
Snow is crisp, and yet
when it warms a little,
snow is wet.

Any winter day, I know,
is pleasanter when there is snow.

Materials

- 34- by 42-inch pocket chart
- 11 sentence strips (6 blue and 5 white)
- snowflake patterns (page 60)
- black marker
- glue
- tagboard
- scissors

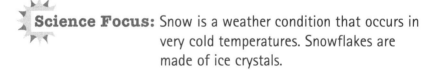

Science Focus: Snow is a weather condition that occurs in very cold temperatures. Snowflakes are made of ice crystals.

Getting Ready

 Write the poem on sentence strips, alternating colors by line.

 Photocopy the snowflake patterns. Then glue them onto tagboard and cut around the shapes.

 Place the sentence strips and snowflakes in the pocket chart.

Reading the Pocket Chart Poem

1 Read the poem aloud once. Then invite children to read it with you.

2 Ask children to point out words in the poem that describe snow, such as *sparkles*, *crunches*, and *cold*.

3 Ask children where they think snow comes from. Explain that snow comes from the clouds. In warm and cold weather, clouds absorb water from the air. When temperatures are warm, the water falls from the clouds as rain. When temperatures are freezing cold, the water turns to ice crystals and falls to Earth as snow.

4 Hold up the six different snowflake patterns. Ask children to tell what is the same about each snowflake (*each has six points*). Then ask them to tell what is different.

5 Ask: "Why are the snowflakes shaped differently?" Remind children that a snowflake is made up of tiny ice crystals that have joined together. No two groups of crystals join together in exactly the same way, so no two snowflakes are exactly the same shape or size.

6 Invite children to read the poem again to find out what happens to snow when the weather grows warmer. Discuss the idea that snow, a solid, melts in warm air and becomes water, a liquid.

Other Ways to Use the Poem

Help children identify the verbs or action words in the poem. Write these on small strips of tagboard. Then help them find the adjectives or describing words. Write these on tagboard as well. Empty the pocket chart. Have children sort the verbs and adjectives, placing them in two separate columns on the chart.

Scramble the order of the sentence strips. Have students work together to place them in the proper order. Then read the poem aloud together.

Beyond the Pocket Chart

If you have already taught the pocket chart on rain (see page 52), you might want to make a Venn diagram to compare rain and snow. To do

this, on the chalkboard, draw two circles that intersect. (See sample, right.) Write *rain* inside one circle and *snow* inside the other. Ask children to give words that tell about each. Write these in the correct circles. Then ask them to tell what is the same about rain and snow (for example, *they are both made of water*). Write these words or comments where the circles overlap.

If snow is available, scoop some into a container and bring it inside. Measure the level of snow in the container. Have children predict the level at which the water will be when the snow melts. Allow the snow to melt, and record observations with the class. Ask: "Which takes up less space: snow or melted snow (water)?"

Use a hand lens to view other kinds of crystals such as sugar, salt, and Epsom salts. These are best viewed when placed on black paper. Encourage children to draw what they see. Then ask them to compare and contrast the different shapes.

ᗯTIPᗯ

If snow is not available, use another form of water in its solid state: ice cubes. Explain to children that ice cubes are also water that has frozen.

Literature

Connections

Bob the Snowman by Sylvia Loretan. (Bohem Press, 1985) A snowman named Bob takes advice from a migrating bird and heads south one winter day. Inevitably, he melts and moves through the water cycle before turning back into snow once again.

Snowballs by Lois Ehlert. (Harcourt Brace Jovanovich, 1995) As children create a snow family, readers learn about snow and how it is formed.

Snow Is Falling by Franklyn Branley. (HarperCollins, 1983) Snow is falling, and there's a lot to learn about it in this informative book for early readers.

The Snowy Day by Ezra Jack Keats. (Puffin, 1978) This well-loved Caldecott winner describes snowfall and its effect on a boy and the world outside his window.

Colors

The Painting Lesson

by Frances Greenwood

Red and blue make purple
Yellow and blue make green.
Such a lot of colors
to paint a lovely scene.
Pink and blue make orchid;
black and white make gray.
Now I'll dry my brushes
until another day.

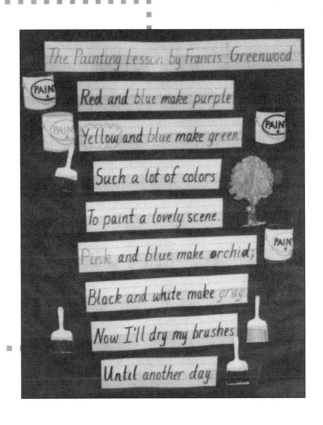

Materials

- 34- by 42-inch pocket chart
- 9 white sentence strips
- colored permanent markers
- patterns (page 64)
- crayons
- glue
- tagboard
- scissors
- chart paper

Science Focus: Colors change when they are mixed together.

Getting Ready

1. Write the poem on sentence strips. Highlight color words by using colored markers on white strips.

2. Make a copy of the tree pattern. Also make four copies each of the paint can and paintbrush patterns. Color each of the paint cans and paintbrushes purple, green, orchid, or gray, as described in the poem. Then glue them onto tagboard and cut them out.

3. Place the sentence strips and patterns in the pocket chart. You may want to use tagboard to cover either the last color word in each sentence or the first two color words in each sentence.

Reading the Pocket Chart Poem

1 Ask your class to name as many colors as they can. Write these on chart paper.

2 Ask children what happens when they are painting and colors mix together.

3 Read the poem aloud. Point to the color words as you name them. If you have covered color words, have children guess the identity of each one before you reveal it.

4 Explain that the color combinations named in the poem are just some of the many ways to mix colors and make new ones. Then reinforce the concept with the activities below.

Other Ways to Use the Poem

Examples of other color combinations include:

red + yellow = orange
brown + white = tan
green + blue = aqua
red + white = pink

⊙ Have children locate the color words in the poem. Write each on its own small strip of tagboard. Make a plus (+) sign on each of four small tagboard strips and a minus (−) sign on four others. Then empty the pocket chart. Place each color combination in the chart as if it is a number sentence (for example, *red + blue = purple*). Encourage children to write other color words on tagboard strips and make their own sentences based on what they know or on class experiments with mixing colors.

⊙ Let children choose one color combination from the poem. Hand out white drawing paper and ask them to use the colors they have chosen to paint a scene that features the two colors and the color they make when combined.

Beyond the Pocket Chart

⊙ Give children hands-on experience in color mixing. Explain that you are going to begin with the primary colors, red, blue, and yellow, because all other colors can be made from these few.

For each child, place a small amount of either red, blue, or yellow paint in a sealable plastic sandwich bag. Then add a different primary color of paint (either red, blue, or yellow). Seal the bag. Instruct children to gently massage the bag to combine the two colors. They will love the results! Then try the following:

- Add a bit of white and black paint to see how the colors lighten and darken.

- Let children dip brushes into the bags and paint on paper, making their own designs or pictures.

Cover a work surface with a plastic tablecloth or old shower curtain. Fill a row of clear plastic cups with water. Add food coloring, dropping a different color in each cup. Mix the water with craft sticks. Let children work in small groups to pour the water into empty cups in various color combinations.

Fill ice cube trays with colored water, varying the colors in each tray. When the cubes freeze, let children place them in cups of warm, colored water. Encourage them to place each cube in water of a different color than the cube. Let children observe and describe the changes that take place as the ice cubes melt.

Set out watercolor paints, brushes, and small cups of clear water. Let children paint freely, observing how paint colors mix on paper and in the water as they dip their brushes.

Place red, yellow, or blue cellophane over the lighted end of a flashlight. Secure with rubber bands. Shine the light onto a white surface. Then overlap colors. Compare what happens when you overlap red and green light to what happens when you mix red and green paint. Then try combining blue and yellow light and blue and yellow paint. You'll find the results surprising!

Connections

Literature

Color Dance by Ann Jonas. (Mulberry Books, 1999) In this fresh, exuberant book, young dancers wave scarves and readers watch what happens when colors combine.

The Color Wizard by Barbara Brenner. (Bantam Doubleday, 1989) Wizard Gray changes his very dull world to a colorful one, in rhyming text and vivid illustrations.

Little Blue and Little Yellow by Leo Lionni. (Astor-Honor, 1959) Two round blobs of color discover how colors combine and separate in this charming story of the power of friendship.

Mouse Paint by Ellen Stoll Walsh. (Harcourt Brace Jovanovich, 1989) Three white mice find jars of blue, red, and yellow paint and discover the world of colors.

Raindrops and Rainbows by Rose Wyler. (Simon & Schuster, 1989) Through simple text and suggested experiments, young readers will learn how clouds and rainbows form.

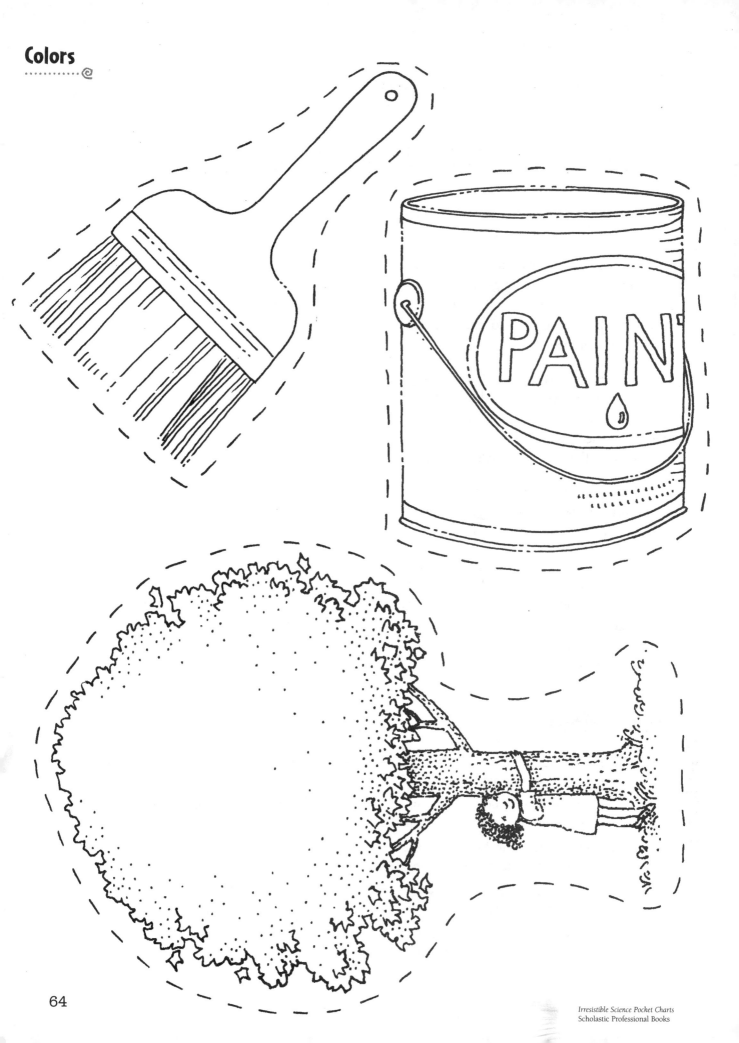